TWO PAN COO[illegible]

For caravans, motor homes,
boats and
other small spaces.

Cheryl Foster

ARMCHER Productions

2 Pan Cooking
First published in Great Britain in 2007
Armcher Productions
PO Box 7098, Blackwell
Alfreton, Derbyshire, DE55 9AR
www.armcher.com

ISBN 978-1-905672-14-1

All recipes in this book have been prepared, cooked, photographed - then consumed - in a camper van!

Printed and bound in China by C&C Offset Printing Co. Ltd.

INDEX OF CONTENTS

2 PAN COOKING

INTRODUCTION

Cooking in a camper, caravan or boat should be part of the fun of being mobile and free from the time consuming maintenance tasks that so beset us when owning a stationary property.

Whilst my husband and I live full time in a camper van, most people are in temporary residence of their mobile home from home. However, which ever category you fall into, the essential task of feeding the family should not become a drudge to be endured whilst everyone else but the cook is having a wonderful time. The meals, so much an enjoyable part of the day should be nutritious, appetising, tasty but easy to prepare and cook.

With very limited work space, complicated techniques or recipes that require a host of pots and pans are to be avoided, replaced by quick, simple cooking requiring as few pans or utensils as possible – with the added bonus that such tactics minimise the washing up!

Mindful of overloading the weight restriction in our camper we fitted ourselves out with gear that was light and compact as possible, thus I brought a camping set of non stick saucepans that consisted of three saucepans, small, medium and large. Within a mere few weeks, the cheap non-stick coating (usually characterised by a very black, shiny, smooth surface) was scratched and peeling not helped by the light, thin pan bottom which made it virtually impossible to cook on the gas without catching and burning food on the bottom - which in turn required hard work to clean off and added to the ruination of the non-stick surface. I quickly dumped the saucepans in favour of proper heavy duty saucepans with decent non-stick coating (usually characterised by a dull almost gritty surface) but mindful of their weight, contented myself with just two pans – one large and one medium sized.

My other cooking equipment consists of a good sized, non stick wok that doubles as frying pan and a non stick roasting/ baking tray. That's it – even if I wanted to go complicated, I couldn't!

Our camper, like most modern British camper vans and caravans, does have a cooker with four gas rings, grill and oven. However, doing a full size Sunday roast, whilst possible, is in my opinion undesirable. It takes too long, uses up too much gas and leaves an awful lot of washing up – none of which is good news in a small space for whilst the cooker may be near full size, the working surfaces and sink certainly are not.

The other cooking equipment we've put on board are two gas rings which on fine days are set up on the camper's table outside. To help keep the wind at bay, we've made a simple 3-sided screen to fit around the 2 burners (some camping stoves have a screen already incorporated in them) and the cooking is done alfresco.

We have friends who spent a year living in a camper. They tried to carry on as if they were in a full size house – including baking their own bread each day – but the effort wore them down. During the summer the camper became too hot and stuffy but they had yet to progress to cooking outside - yet cooking in the open, glass of wine at hand is surely one of life's pleasures.

Bearing all this in mind, I quickly adapted my normal recipes to fit the constraints of a camper/caravan environment so that in the main the recipes I employ use only two pans and whilst they can easily be cooked on top of the stove, just as importantly, they can readily transfer to cooking outside.

When cooking outside I try to get all the necessary ingredients for the meal together at the start so as to minimize the number of times I have to re-climb aboard the van to fetch something and whilst invariably there is always something one forgets, a couple of minutes spent collecting all the ingredients on a tray helps cut down on unwanted journeys.

The name of the game is to produce tasty, delicious and nutritious meals with the minimum of preparation and difficulty. It is my absolute belief that the cook should be able to enjoy the food as much as anyone and not end up being too hot and bothered to eat. To this end the recipes shown here are simple, quick and take on average 15 minutes to prepare and 30/45 minutes to cook – just long enough to have that aperitif!

BASIC KITCHEN EQUIPMENT

When I first came to camping, I tried bringing my whole kitchen with me. My husband - used to a lot more basic 'back pack' camping - soon pared down the utensils so that they fitted into the one draw allocated for the task but even from this I have learnt that in fact I use very few utensils, reducing down to:

Small chopping board – durable plastic for lightness
Small all purpose kitchen knife
Large all purpose kitchen knife - which doubles as bread knife
2 x wooden spoons
1 plastic coated draining spoon
1 plastic coated fish spatula
Potato peeler
Small whisk
Set of measuring spoons
Tin opener
Knife sharpener
Sieve that doubles as a strainer
Plastic measuring jug
Spatula
Pastry brush

Plus the most used item in my kitchen –
A bottle opener!

Besides the utensils and in addition to the cooking equipment mentioned in the *Introduction*, I also carry 1 large and 2 medium sized plastic mixing bowls with lids, which double as serving dishes when required. I have also acquired along the way several plastic tubs of the Chinese takeaway variety, which I find very useful for left overs in the fridge or for putting ingredients in for cooking outdoors.
That's my kitchen equipment and despite a love of all things 'kitcheny', I try very hard not to add to the list despite frequent temptation!

BASIC LARDER

My basic larder is controlled by both the space available and the amount of weight I can squeeze out from the overall restriction on the camper van. Tins and glass are heavy but I try to maintain a store of basics over and above the weekly consumed items such as fresh fruit, meat and vegetables.

In the cupboard

Bottle of virgin olive oil
Tin chopped tomatoes
Tin kidney beans
Tin baked beans
Tin mushrooms
Tin sliced green beans
Tin sweet corn
Tin of new potatoes
Tin or packet coconut milk/cream
Small packet plain flour
Small packet of caster sugar
Jar of sweetener powder
Packet of sultanas
Tube of tomato puree
Tin of ham
Eggs
Tub of 'parmesan' cheese
Bottle Worcester sauce
Bottle Soy sauce
Bottle Tabasco sauce
Dried spices & herbs: Garlic powder
Mixed herbs
Chilli powder
Ginger powder
Curry powder
Garam masala
Paprika

Cayenne pepper
Turmeric
Salt
Ground black pepper

Jar of mustard
Onions
Packet of rice
Packet of pasta
Potatoes
Tea
Coffee
UHT packets of milk

As I do have an oven, I also try and keep several packets of part-baked bread rolls in the larder as a standby if I run out of fresh bread. These can have a shelf life of over 2 months.

Fridge-Freezer

Our camper has 80 litre capacity fridge/freezer with a freezer compartment measuring 36 cm x 14 cm x 18 cm (14"x 5½" x 7"). Nevertheless I can pack away meat for five main meals (the meat, of course, is taken out of its bulky packaging and stored in freezer bags) plus a 450 gms packet of frozen peas, packet of frozen prawns and a small packet of another frozen vegetable within its small confines. Luckily we don't eat ice-cream which would probably spoil this fine feat of engineering!
The fridge itself (always too small at the beginning of the week!) can have besides the weekly replenishment of more fresh meat, salad, yogurt, etc., a tub of margarine, bottle concentrated lemon juice, jam and marmalade, tomato ketchup, mayonnaise and a bottle of (oil free) salad dressing.
My aim is to try to take on board sufficient shopping for at least a week at a time as I don't want to have to keep unplugging the van to go and find suitable shops but it does require you to have at least a rough idea of the menu for the week ahead.

NOTES

As it is essential that my husband keeps his weight in check, my cooking is now virtually fat-free and sugar free - the sugar replaced by sweeteners - but remains (to us anyway!) tasty and this regime is reflected in the recipes given. I use very little additional cooking oil – just enough to grease the bottom of the non-stick pan - and either trim off fat or remove the skin from meat to reduce the intake of fat but this is a personal choice and you can, of course, use more oil than suggested, elect to keep the skin or fat on the meat and use sugar as stated in the recipes.

This low use of oil is applied when cooking onions. With just a teaspoon of oil, the oil is heated then the onions added. The heat is immediately turned down to its lowest setting, a lid put on and the onions allowed to sweat gently until soft. However, you may prefer to use a little more oil than stated in the recipes and fry the onions until soft &/or brown according to your own tastes.

I no longer cook dishes with cream but I have included some old favourites, especially suited for entertaining and special occasions. These days if I do a recipe that includes cream, I substitute a couple of generous tablespoons of low fat crème fraîche instead.

Again with an eye on dietary requirements, you may, like us, prefer to substitute chicken or turkey mince instead of beef mince.

When it comes to taste, do use the amount of spices, especially in the curried recipes, as a guide only - remember it is you, not the cookbook that is eating the dish, so it's your personal taste that counts. Also I've found different brands of curry powder vary a great deal in taste and strength so you may find it necessary to try several to find the one that suits you and it may be prudent to start with the lesser amounts quoted in the recipes and add extra as you go along.

Over the last few years I have reduced our intake of salt too so you may find that you require more salt than the measurements given. You should in any event always taste the food before serving and adjust accordingly, remembering that you can always add but you cannot take away!

If fresh ingredients such as garlic and mushrooms are available to you, so much the better but life in a camper/caravan/boat is not about spending vast amounts of time shopping – food shopping any way! – so for convenience as well as for the important aspect of space and weight, I use garlic powder and have pared down the number of spices and herbs I carry – for instance mixed herbs are substituted for every other kind of herb required and curry powder is used instead of blends of individual spices – and I use dried herbs and spices as the norm, with the exception of parsley which is either fresh or not used at all!

Likewise I keep just Virgin Olive Oil in the larder and have come down to one packet of pasta at any one time – although it is of course always possible to buy packets of fresh pasta for a particular recipe, such as tagliatelle, when shopping.

When we can, we stop off at farm shops (especially for strawberries and raspberries when in season!) but in the main we take our 23 foot camper to supermarkets, if possible very early in the morning thereby hopefully avoiding getting boxed in by other cars.

Finally, unless otherwise stated, teaspoons and tablespoon measures are level spoonfuls.

BEEF & GROUNDNUT STEW

A combination of beef and groundnuts (monkey nuts) makes this an unusual dish to serve but it tastes wonderful - especially when accompanied by fried bananas! - and although it takes about an hour and a half to cook, it is well worth the time it takes.

This dish can be served with rice or potatoes - try mashed to soak up the delicious gravy!

INGREDIENTS

Potatoes or rice of choice.

2 teaspoons olive oil
450 gms (1lb) stewing steak, cut into 1" cubes
1 large onion, thinly sliced
1 green pepper, sliced
Large tin of chopped tomatoes
100 gms (4oz) roasted groundnuts (monkey nuts),
shelled & skinned
1 beef stock cube
175 ml (6 fl. oz) water
1 teaspoon salt
¼ teaspoon pepper
¼ teaspoon cayenne pepper
1 teaspoon mixed herbs

METHOD

In a large pan, heat 1 teaspoon of oil, add the meat cubes to seal and brown.
Remove the meat from the pan and if necessary use the remaining oil before adding the onions and peppers.
Fry for 5/6 minutes.
Stir in the tomatoes, return the meat to the pan, add the nuts, beef stock cube, water, salt, pepper, cayenne and herbs.
Bring the liquid to the boil then with lid on, reduce heat to low and simmer for 1 hour or until the meat is tender.
If necessary, add a little more water to the stock whilst cooking.
Use your second pan to cook the potatoes or rice.

NOTE
If you want to serve this dish with fried bananas, at the end of cooking time, transfer the stew into a serving bowl (place saucepan lid on top to help keep warm), wipe out the pan and cook the bananas (see recipe page 101). This should take less than 5 minutes.

CHILLI CON CARNE

Along with Spaghetti Bolognaise, this is an oldie but a goodie. Served on a bed of plain boiled rice, a side salad goes well with this dish but so does that hot garlic bread!

Remember that a pot of chilli powder is much more potent when first opened than when several weeks old so treat new chilli with caution, especially if you have been getting liberal with your old chilli because you consider it has lost its 'oomph'!

INGREDIENTS

Plain boiled rice cooked as per packet instructions

1 teaspoon olive oil
450 gms (1 lb) lean minced beef
1 onion, chopped
1-2 teaspoons chilli powder
½ teaspoon mixed herbs
1 teaspoon garlic powder
Large can of chopped tomatoes
1-2 tablespoons tomato puree
Large can red kidney beans (drained and rinsed)
½ teaspoon salt
⅛ teaspoon ground black pepper

METHOD

Heat the oil in a large saucepan then add the chopped onions, gently cooking until soft.
Add the meat and brown.
Add the chilli powder (I suggest one teaspoon to start unless you are sure you like it hot), the herbs, garlic, tomatoes, 1 tablespoon tomato puree, kidney beans, salt and pepper.
Stir, bring to boil then lower the heat to simmer, cover and cook 30/40 minutes.
Meanwhile, using the second pan, cook the rice as per packet instructions.
When the rice and chilli are ready, taste the chilli and if necessary add more chilli powder for that extra 'bite' or tomato puree if the sauce needs thickening or enriching. You may also require a little extra salt to taste.
Drain rice and serve.

Note
If you have some chilli con carne left over, or if you fancy a change from rice, use it as a topping to a jacket potato OR on top of a couple of slices of bread.

MEATBALL CURRY

This takes a little time to prepare but I find making the meatballs very therapeutic and it's a very tasty way of using mince.
Serve with plain boiled rice and coriander naan bread.
As usual with curries, I top this curry with 'small chop' (see recipe 120).
I use a teaspoon of hot chilli powder in both the meatballs and the sauce but this does produce a fairly hot dish, so you may prefer to use ½ teaspoon each time.

INGREDIENTS

Plain boiled rice cooked as per instructions on packet

Meatballs:
500 gms (1 lb) lean minced beef
3 tablespoons plain flour
1 level teaspoon ground ginger
1 teaspoon garlic powder
½ - 1 teaspoon hot chilli powder
1 teaspoon salt
½ teaspoon turmeric
1 egg (beaten)
1 small onion, finely chopped
1 teaspoon olive oil

Sauce:
1 teaspoon olive oil
1 onion, finely chopped
1 level teaspoon ground ginger
1 teaspoon garlic powder
½ - 1 teaspoon hot chilli powder
2 tablespoons garam masala) or 1 can coconut milk
1 inch cream coconut)
450 ml (16 fl. oz) water
1 teaspoon salt

METHOD

First make the sauce.
In one pan, heat the oil then gently cook the onions until soft.
Add the ginger, garlic powder, chilli powder and garam masala and fry for 5 minutes, adding a spoonful of water if too dry.
Add the salt, coconut cream and water (or can of coconut milk) to the pan. Bring to the boil and simmer for 15 minutes whilst you make the meatballs.

Put all the meatball ingredients except the oil into a large bowl.
Using a fork, mix well then shape into approximately 24 walnut sized balls.
Heat the remaining oil in the second pan (I use my wok) and fry the meatballs 4/5 minutes, moving them about to make sure they brown evenly. You may need to do this in 2 or 3 batches.
As the meatballs are browned, add them to the sauce.
When all the meatballs have been added, bring the mixture to the boil, turn the heat down, cover and simmer for a further 30 minutes.
In the meantime, wash out the second pan and use it to cook the rice.
When the rice and meatballs are ready, taste the sauce and if necessary add a little more seasoning.
Serve.

MEATBALLS IN TOMATO SAUCE with PASTA

This could be described as a more sophisticated version of spaghetti bolognese and I have certainly served it to great acclaim at dinner parties.

The preparation does take a little time but you can make the meatballs in advance and it more than pays you back with the final result!

This dish could be served with any pasta you have to hand. Spaghetti is probably the most usual but I often use penne - it's a lot easier to eat especially if you are outside eating on laps!

If you don't already do so, try serving up in bowls rather than plates. Again, it makes it a lot easier to eat.

INGREDIENTS

Pasta of choice, cooked as per packet instructions

Meatballs:
2 slices of bread, crusts cut off
60 ml (2 fl. oz) milk
450 gms (1 lb) lean minced beef
25 gms (1 oz) parmesan cheese
1 small egg (beaten)
½ teaspoon salt
¼ teaspoon black pepper
1 teaspoon mixed herbs
1 teaspoon garlic powder
1 teaspoon olive oil

Tomato Sauce:
1 teaspoon olive oil
1 onion, chopped
1 teaspoon garlic powder
Large tin of chopped tomatoes
50 gms (2 oz) tomato puree
½ teaspoon salt
¼ teaspoon black pepper
½ teaspoon mixed herbs
1 teaspoon sugar (or sweetener)

Garnish (optional)
Parmesan cheese

METHOD

First make the sauce.
In one pan, heat the oil and cook the onions until soft but not brown.
Add the garlic, chopped tomatoes, tomato puree, salt, pepper, mixed herbs and sugar.

Stir well, bring to the boil, cover then simmer whilst you make the meatballs.
In a large mixing bowl, lightly beat the egg into the milk then soak the bread in the liquid. When it is soft, mash it up then add the remaining meatball ingredients, except the oil.
Using a fork, mix well then shape into approximately 24 walnut size balls. If the mixture seems a little wet, sprinkle over some plain flour and mix well in.
Heat the oil in a large pan (I use my wok) then fry the meatballs 4-5 minutes until evenly brown. You may have to do 2-3 batches.
As you brown the meatballs, add them to the sauce and when all the meatballs have been added, bring the mixture to the boil then lower the heat, recover and simmer for a further 30 minutes.
In the meantime, wash the spare pan out and use it to cook the pasta.
Before serving, taste for seasoning.
Serve the meatballs on a bed of pasta with a sprinkle of parmesan cheese on top.

MEXICAN STUFFED PEPPERS

Hot and spicy, the original recipe had the peppers cooked in the oven topped with a cheese, cream and sultana sauce.
I have adapted the recipe to cook on the top and mindful of my husband's waist line, substituted the cream & cheese sauce with a sprinkle of parmesan cheese at the end. Works for us!

INGREDIENTS

Plain boiled rice cooked as per packet instructions

1 teaspoon olive oil
3 peppers – green, yellow or red as you prefer
1 onion, chopped
1 teaspoon garlic powder
1 teaspoon hot chilli powder
450 gms (1 lb) lean minced beef
1 teaspoon herbs
1 teaspoon salt
1-2 tablespoons flour
225 ml (8 oz) water
1 beef stock cube
110 gms (4 oz) sultanas

(Optional)
1 generous tablespoon of (low fat) crème fraîche
Parmesan cheese

METHOD

Slice 1" from the top of each pepper and dice into small pieces. Discard seeds and pith and if necessary slice off a little of the bottom of the peppers to ensure that they sit upright.
Heat the oil in a large pan. Add the onion and cook until soft but not brown. Add the beef and fry until the beef begins to brown.
Stir in 1 tablespoon of flour then add the water and stock and bring to the boil.
Add the diced pieces of pepper, herbs, salt, garlic, chilli powder and sultanas, reduce the heat to simmer, cover the pan and cook for 15 minutes.

At the end of this time, stir in the crème fraîche.
Fill the prepared peppers with the beef mixture and place back into the pan, leaving a residue of meat mixture in the pan to ensure that the peppers do not stick or burn in a dry pan. (If necessary, add a little water.)
Cook for a further 30 minutes or until the peppers are soft when pierced with a knife. If the 'gravy' of the remaining beef mixture is too thin at the end, carefully sprinkle and stir in some more flour.
In the meantime, cook the rice in the second pan.
When cooked, place the peppers on a bed of rice, spoon the rest of the mixture around the peppers and sprinkle some parmesan cheese on top.
Serve.

Note
For a quicker version of the above or if you are not keen on eating a whole pepper, chop just one pepper into small chunks and add it all at the beginning of the recipe (at the same time as the herbs, salt, garlic, etc.). Cook the dish for 30 minutes and serve with the rice.

SPAGHETTI BOLOGNESE

I can remember when serving spaghetti bolognese to guests was the height of sophistication and although it has lost a little of its 'glamour' recently, I still think this dish is well worth having in your repertoire as it is quick, easy, inexpensive and still tastes good!

INGREDIENTS

Spaghetti (or pasta of choice) cooked according to the packet instructions

1 teaspoon of olive oil
1 onion, chopped
1 teaspoon garlic powder
450 gms (1 lb) lean mince beef
Large can of chopped tomatoes
½ teaspoon mixed herbs
1 teaspoon Worcester sauce
2 tablespoons tomato puree
110 gms sliced mushrooms or small tin of sliced mushrooms
1 teaspoon sugar (sweetener)
1 teaspoon salt
¼ teaspoon pepper

Garnish (Optional)
Grated Parmesan cheese

METHOD

Heat the oil in a saucepan and add the onion.
Cook until the onion is soft but not brown.
Add the beef and brown the meat.
Add the chopped tomatoes, mixed herbs, Worcester sauce, tomato puree, mushrooms, salt, pepper and sugar (sweetener).
Bring to the boil, lower the heat to simmer, cover and cook 30/35 minutes.
Using the second pan, cook the pasta as per the instructions on the packet.
When the pasta and sauce are ready, taste the sauce and if necessary add a little more seasoning if required.
Serve the sauce on the bed of pasta and before eating, sprinkle over the parmesan cheese.

STIR FRIED BEEF with BEAN SPROUTS

This is a very quick stir fry meal. Malay rather than Chinese in influence, it has the 'oriental' ingredients of soy sauce, ginger, garlic and sugar.

This dish can be served with plain boiled rice or noodles.

INGREDIENTS

Rice or noodles of choice, cooked as per packet instructions.

3 tablespoons soy sauce
1 teaspoon garlic powder
2 teaspoon cornflour
1 teaspoon sugar (or sweetener)
680 gms (1½ lbs) rump steak, thinly sliced and cut into strips
1 tablespoon olive oil
1½ teaspoon ground ginger
Large tin (225 gms/8 oz) bean sprouts

METHOD

In a bowl, combine the soy sauce, garlic, cornflour, ginger and sugar (sweetener). Mix in the beef strips. Leave to marinate for at least half an hour.
In one pan, cook the rice or noodles according to the instructions on the packet.
Ten minutes from the end of cooking time, heat the oil in a large pan or wok .
Add the beef mixture, including liquid, and cook for 5 minutes.
Add the bean sprouts and continue to fry for a further 3 minutes.
Taste for seasoning but I find I do not need to add any salt or pepper. Remember, soy sauce has salt in its ingredients.
Serve.

CHICKEN MADELEINE

This is a rich chicken dish as it uses cream and oil in the sauce but this dish was a dinner party speciality of my Mother-in-Law. All of her friends begged her for the recipe but she refused to give it to anyone. However, I'm willing to share the secret of this delicious dish. If the ingredients seem an odd mixture, don't be put off. They work beautifully together.

To reduce the fat content, I have substituted single cream for the original double cream and you can substitute even this with low fat crème fraîche depending on your dietary requirements.

You should serve this dish with plain boiled rice and peas.

INGREDIENTS

Plain boiled rice cooked as per packet instructions with
225 (8 oz peas) added towards the end of cooking time.

Chicken breasts - at least 1 per person
1 teaspoon olive oil

Sauce
1 teaspoon English mustard powder (or 1 teaspoon ready made)
2 teaspoons sugar or sweetener
3 teaspoons curry powder
8 tablespoons tomato ketchup
4 tablespoons olive oil
2 tablespoons (light) vinegar
1 teaspoon salt
150 ml (5 fl. oz) cream (double, single or low fat crème fraîche).

METHOD

Heat the teaspoon of oil in a saucepan and coat the bottom of the pan with it.
Skin the chicken pieces (or leave the skin on if you prefer) and add to saucepan. Fry gently to seal the chicken then cover the pan, keep on low heat and cook the chicken in its own juices, turning frequently to ensure even cooking and to avoid the chicken sticking to the pan.
In the meantime make the sauce by adding all the sauce ingredients, other than the cream and salt, into the second pan.
Stirring all the time to mix well, slowly heat the mixture.
When it is hot but not boiling, add the cream, a little at a time.
Taste as you go until the sauce is rich and creamy enough for you.
Add salt to taste (but I generally do not need any).

When the chicken is cooked, either place in a casserole dish and spoon over the sauce or add the sauce direct to the chicken pan. Leave to fuse on low heat either in the oven if using a casserole dish or on top in the saucepan – but try not to let the sauce boil – whilst you cook the rice and peas. The dish can stay in the oven for anything up to an hour without spoiling thus making it an ideal dish if you are entertaining.
Wash out the sauce pan and use it to cook the rice and peas.

Note
If you are partial to prawns, this sauce goes down well with them too. The recipe is exactly the same except you substitute 450 gms (1 lb) prawns for the chicken.

CHICKEN with PRAWNS and ASPARAGUS

There's more than a hint of luxury to this dish which is special enough to serve at a dinner party. However, there is no reason why you should not eat this dish at any time as it is very straight forward to prepare. Serve with potatoes and peas.

INGREDIENTS

Potatoes
200 gms (7 oz) peas

1 teaspoon olive oil
1 chicken, cut into 8 serving pieces (or chicken breasts or thighs)
1 onion finely chopped
3 tablespoons flour
420 ml (15 fl. oz) water
1 chicken stock cube
1 teaspoon salt
¼ teaspoon pepper
¼ teaspoon paprika
Pinch of mixed herbs
Large can of asparagus (cut)
225 gms (8 oz) prawns
150 ml (5 fl. oz) cream or 2 generous
tablespoons of (low fat) crème fraîche)

METHOD

Heat the olive oil in large pan. Skin (or not!) the chicken pieces then add to the pan and brown. Remove.
Add the chopped onion to the pan and cook until soft, adding a little more oil if necessary.
Stir in the flour then gradually add the water.
Add the salt, pepper, paprika, stock cube, herbs plus the chicken and bring to the boil. Lower heat and simmer for 30 minutes.
Stir in the asparagus and prawns.
At the same time, in a second pan, start cooking the potatoes.
Cook the chicken dish for another 15 minutes (or until the chicken is cooked) then remove the chicken pieces into a serving bowl.
Add the peas to the potato pan.
Stir the cream (crème fraîche) into the chicken sauce, stirring constantly for 2/3 minutes until the sauce is hot but not boiling. Check for seasoning then pour the sauce over the chicken.
Serve.

CHICKEN WITH RICE

This is a wonderful ONE PAN meal that is very easy to cook and simply delicious! If you want to ruin the low fat goodness of the meal and have the means to heat it up, serve with hot garlic bread.

INGREDIENTS

1 teaspoon of olive oil
6 slices of bacon, chopped
Large packet of chicken thighs
1 onion, chopped
Large tin chopped tomatoes
2 teaspoons of paprika
1/8 teaspoon of saffron or 1 teaspoon turmeric (to colour the rice yellow)
175 gms (6 oz) long grain rice
Water
150 gms (5 oz) frozen peas
1 teaspoon garlic powder
1 teaspoon of salt

Garnish (optional)
2 tablespoons freshly chopped parsley

METHOD

Remove the skin from the chicken pieces and if you wish, de-bone and cut the chicken into pieces. You can, if you wish, keep the skin on but that does of course add to the fat content of the dish.
Heat the oil in a wok or large pan then fry the bacon.
When lightly cooked, remove and set aside.
Add the onion to the pan and cook until the onion is soft.
Add the chicken pieces and seal the meat before re-adding the bacon together with the garlic, tomatoes, paprika, saffron (or turmeric) and salt. Bring to the boil, lower the heat and cook for 5 minutes.
Add the rice and stir well to mix. Bring the pan back to the boil then turn the heat down to simmering, cover the pan with a lid and cook for 30 minutes.

Stir the contents once or twice during the cooking time to ensure that the food does not stick on the bottom and also to check that there is sufficient liquid for the rice to cook.
If necessary, add water. The amount of water required will depend on the liquid content of your tin of tomatoes. (The cheaper tins of chopped tomato usually have more liquid in them than their dearer counterparts but work just as well in this dish - you simply do not need to add as much water.) At the end of the cooking time, the water should be absorbed into the rice so if needed, add just a little water each time to avoid the dish becoming too wet.
Add the peas and cook for a further 10 minutes or until the rice is cooked and has absorbed the water.
Sprinkle with chopped parsley and serve.

COLONIAL CHICKEN CURRY

We love curries and this recipe is our favourite. Chicken and curry just go together superbly.

When I had a full sized kitchen, my spice range was much larger and I used to blend the different spices together but now I just use curry powder and garam masala. Seems to work just as well! If you are not fond of hot curries or are unsure, exchange the hot curry powder for medium and use the lower measurements – adding more if required. Remember you can add but you cannot take away!

In Kenya where my husband grew up, curries were accompanied by bowls of 'small chop' - highly recommended! - see page 120.

INGREDIENTS

Plain boiled rice (cooked as per packet instructions)

1 teaspoon of olive oil
Packet of chicken thighs – for ease of eating we generally take
the chicken off the bone and chop it into bite size pieces
1 large onion – chopped
Large can of chopped tomatoes
1 teaspoon of salt
1 teaspoon garlic powder
2 tablespoons (hot) curry powder
2 tablespoons garam masala
50 gms (2 oz) of sultanas
½ inch slice of creamed coconut or 1/3 tin of coconut milk
(stirred to blend the thin & thick part of the milk)

METHOD

Heat oil in large saucepan then add the chopped onions, cooking until soft.
Add 2 tablespoons of curry power and 2 tablespoons of garam masala and mix well with the onions. Let the mixture 'fry' for a couple of minutes, stirring to stop the mixture sticking then add the tin of chopped tomatoes and stir well.
Add the garlic and salt then the chicken pieces and sultanas. Stir to ensure the chicken is coated with the sauce, bring to the boil then lowering the heat to simmer, cover and cook for 40 minutes or until the chicken is tender.
In the meantime, using the second pan, cook the rice so that it is ready at the same time as the curry.
When the curry is ready, add the coconut cream/milk. This smoothes the curry sauce and is a great bonus but because of this, don't be tempted to put too much in – over do it and the coconut instead of enhancing, deadens the spice flavour and spoils the curry.

Now taste the curry for strength and flavour. If heat and flavour is required, add some more curry powder. If the curry is hot enough but needs a little more flavour add some garam masala. However, if only heat is required, try a little hot chilli powder.

Remember don't add in tablespoons at a time, you could well over do it. Try just half a tablespoon (or ½ teaspoon in the case of the chilli powder) and taste again once you have stirred well. You might also need to add a little more salt. It's not a precise art as everyone's taste buds are different!

Note
If you don't have any coconut cream/milk, try 2 tablespoons of natural yogurt stirred in at the end of the cooking time after taking the pan off the heat (thus minimizing the likelihood of the yogurt curdling).

MEDITERRANEAN CHICKEN

This dish is very easy to prepare and if the chicken is skinned, virtually fat free. Using the colour and taste of Mediterranean vegetables – tomatoes, courgettes and aubergine in particular – the vegetables become almost like ratatouille.
Serve the dish with either rice or potatoes.

Note
Although the recipe uses chicken thighs, you can use a whole chicken but you will need to increase the cooking time. Simply place the whole chicken (with or without skin and without giblets) on top of the tomatoes and proceed as given, allowing minimum of 20 minutes cooking time per ½ kilo (1 lb). Test the chicken to see if it is cooked by inserting the tip of a knife into the flesh. If the liquid runs clear, it is ready. If it shows pink, cook the chicken a little longer.

INGREDIENTS

Rice or potatoes as preferred

Large packet of chicken thighs
1 medium onion, chopped in half and thickly sliced
1 leek, cut lengthways in half and then sliced into ¼" thick pieces
2 courgettes, cut lengthways in half and chopped into chunks
1 aubergine, cut lengthways then chopped into chunks
1 large red, green or yellow pepper, cut into wide strips (optional)
Large can of chopped tomatoes
100 gms (4 oz) fresh mushrooms, sliced or small tin of sliced mushrooms
½ teaspoon herbs
1 teaspoon garlic powder
1 teaspoon salt
¼ teaspoon black pepper
1-2 tablespoons tomato puree

METHOD

Empty the tin of tomatoes into a large, deep pan or wok.
Skin (and if preferred, bone) the chicken and place the thighs on top of the tomatoes.
Arrange the onion, leek, courgettes, aubergines, mushrooms and peppers on top of the chicken. Sprinkle with herbs, garlic, salt and pepper.
Bring to the boil, lower heat to simmer and cover. Cook for 45 minutes or until the chicken is tender and the vegetables have cooked down.
Stir the ingredients from time to time so that they cook evenly, checking that nothing sticks to the bottom of the pan.
Approximately 20/25 minutes from the end of the cooking time, use the second pan to cook the rice or potatoes.
At the end of the cooking time, add the tomato puree to the vegetable mixture to enrich and thicken the sauce.
Taste, adjusting seasoning as required and serve.

RED CHICKEN

As its name suggests, this dish is deep red in colour due to the strong tomato content. However the paprika and cayenne pepper gives it quite a bite and lifts the sauce from being just plain tomato.
Serve the dish with potatoes or rice and peas.

INGREDIENTS

Rice or potatoes as preferred
225 gms (8 oz) peas

1 teaspoon of olive oil
2 tablespoons of seasoned flour:
    2 tablespoons plain flour,
    1 teaspoon salt,
    ¼ teaspoon pepper
    1 teaspoon garlic powder
Large packet of chicken thighs
50 gms (2 oz) mushrooms, sliced or small tin sliced mushrooms
I large onion, chopped
Chicken stock cube
150 ml (5 fl. oz)) water
Large tin of chopped tomatoes) If you don't have a tin of tomatoes
1 tablespoon tomato puree) use 150 gms (5 oz) tomato puree
) and add a little extra water
Green pepper, deseeded and sliced (optional)
2 teaspoons paprika
¼ level teaspoon cayenne pepper
½ teaspoon salt
½ teaspoon garlic powder
½ teaspoon dried herbs

METHOD

Heat the oil in a large saucepan (I use my wok), add the onions and gently cook until soft.
Make up the seasoned flour in a plastic bag.
Skin the chicken and place in the bag, shake, ensuring an even coating of the seasoned flour then add the chicken pieces to the pan, allowing them to lightly brown. It may be necessary to do this in two lots.

Add the tomatoes, puree, mushrooms, herbs, garlic, stock cube, water, salt, paprika, cayenne pepper and green pepper if using.
Stir and bring to the boil, cover and simmer for 40 minutes or until the chicken is tender.
Approximately 20/25minutes from the end of cooking time, cook the rice or potatoes adding the peas 5 minutes before serving.
Test the chicken dish for taste and add additional seasoning if necessary. If the sauce is too thin, mix any remaining seasoned flour (or some flour/cornflour) with a little water and stir into the pan a little at a time, continuing until the sauce is the required thickness.
Serve.

SPICEY CHICKEN

There is a rich, creamy smoothness to this easy to prepare dish which I often serve at dinner parties whether in the camper van or not! Although the chicken is tossed in spices, the dish is not hot nor is it a curry.

Serve with potatoes and peas or green beans.

INGREDIENTS

Potatoes
225 gms (8 oz) peas or green beans

Seasoned flour made up of: 75 gms (3 oz) plain flour
1 teaspoon paprika
2 teaspoons turmeric
1 teaspoon cayenne pepper
2 tablespoons garam masala
1 teaspoon salt

1 tablespoon olive oil
8 pieces chicken (legs, thighs or drum sticks)
1 large onion, chopped
1 teaspoon ginger
4 tablespoons of apple puree (or finely chopped desert apple)
150 ml (5 fl. oz) single cream (or 2 tablespoons crème fraîche)
450 ml (16 fl. oz) water
1 chicken stock cube
2 teaspoons soft brown sugar (1 teaspoon sweetener)

METHOD

Make up the seasoned flour in a plastic bag.
Skin the chicken pieces– you can leave the skin on if you prefer - then coat with the seasoned flour . Retain remaining flour.
Heat half the oil in a pan then cook the onions until soft.
Remove onions from the pan and add the chicken pieces to brown, adding the remaining oil as necessary.
Return the onions to the pan and add the apple puree, ginger, water, stock cube and sugar (sweetener). Bring to the boil then simmer for 40 minutes.
Approximately 25 minutes from the end of the cooking time, use your second pan to cook the potatoes, adding the peas/beans 5 minutes before serving.
In small bowl blend the remaining flour with water then stirring all the time, slowly add to the casserole until the sauce is thick.
Taste and if necessary add a little more salt.
Stir in the cream (crème fraîche) and serve.

DUCK BREASTS WITH MUSHROOM & CAPER SAUCE

Packets of duck breasts are widely available on the Continent but can now be seen in the larger supermarkets in Britain. It is delicious, but as you cook the duck with the fat on (then remove it before serving) it does spit quite a lot so this is an ideal dish to cook OUTDOORS to avoid fat splashes and cooking smells indoors.
Serve the duck with potatoes and cut green beans (or green vegetable of choice) cooked together in one pan.

INGREDIENTS

Boiled potatoes with or without the skin left on.
Cut green beans - or green vegetable of choice.

1 duck breast (with fat on) per person
Small tin of sliced mushrooms
Small tin of capers (optional)
150 ml (5 fl. oz) single cream (or 2 generous heaped tablespoons crème fraîche)
Salt and pepper to taste

METHOD

In one pan, cook the potatoes.
Score the fat side of the duck breasts with three or four deep slashes.
Put second pan - a wok if it has a lid is ideal - over a medium heat and when hot, place the duck breasts, fat side down, in the pan.
Cover the pan and leave to cook on medium heat for 8 minutes.
Do not add any fat/oil to the pan.
After cooking for eight minutes, turn the duck breasts over and continue to cook for a further 5 minutes.
Be careful as there will be a lot of hot fat in the pan and it is very easy to splash it everywhere when turning the duck over!
Add the cut green beans or alternative vegetable to the potato pan.
Remove the duck breasts from the pan and keep warm - place on a plate and cover with the lid of the pan - whilst you quickly make the sauce.
Pour the fat out of the pan, leaving just the duck juice in the pan. (I pour the fat into a cup and allow the fat to solidify before discarding in the waste bin. I do not recommend pouring the hot fat directly down the sink.)
Add the mushrooms and capers and cook for 2/3 minutes then add the cream (crème fraîche) to the pan and stir well. Allow the sauce to heat up and thicken.

Remove any remaining fat from the duck breasts, season with salt and pepper and carve diagonally before placing on a plate.
Spoon over the sauce.
Drain the potatoes and vegetables and serve.

Note
If not restricted to 2 pans, try this dish with Belgian Roast Potatoes (see page 115) or oven chips.

BELL PEPPER LAMB MEATBALLS

A little preparation time is required to make the meatballs but its well worth it for this tasty way to serve minced lamb.
The meatballs are cooked in their own tomato based sauce and served with pasta of choice.
An optional extra is to sprinkle parmesan cheese over the dish at the time of serving.

INGREDIENTS

Pasta of choice, cooked as per packet instructions

450 gms (1 lb) minced lamb
1 medium size onion
1 green pepper
1 small egg, lightly beaten
2 tablespoons plain flour
2 x ½ teaspoon salt
2 x ¼ teaspoon pepper
2 x 1 teaspoon garlic powder
½ teaspoon dried mixed herbs
1 teaspoon sugar (sweetener)
5 oz tomato puree
125 ml (1/4 pt) water
2 x 1 teaspoon olive oil.

Garnish
Parmesan cheese (optional)

METHOD

Put the lamb into a mixing bowl.
Take one third of the onion and one third of the green pepper and dice very fine.
Add to the lamb together with ½ teaspoon salt, ¼ teaspoon pepper and 1 teaspoon of garlic then sprinkle over the flour, add the egg and with a fork, thoroughly blend the mixture.
Dice the remaining onion and pepper.
Heat a teaspoon of olive oil in a medium size saucepan and add the remaining peppers and onion.
Turn down heat to minimum; put a lid on and let the onions & peppers sweat until they have softened.

Keep an eye on the mixture to make sure it does not stick or brown.
In the meantime, using you hands, make the lamb mixture into walnut size meatballs.
Heat the remaining oil in the second pan and add the meatballs – one layer at a time – and brown.
Whilst the first lot of meatballs are browning, add the tomato puree, water, mixed herbs, remaining salt, pepper, garlic and the teaspoon of sugar (sweetener) to the onion & pepper mixture in the first pan.
Stir well and bring to the boil then simmer with the lid on for 40 minutes, adding the meatballs as they brown.
Discard the fat from the second pan and wash out ready to cook the pasta.
Cook the pasta according to the packet instructions so that it is ready at the same time as the meatballs.
Before serving, skim off any excess fat from the meatball mixture then taste the meatball sauce and adjust for seasoning if required.
Serve with a bowl of parmesan cheese on the side.

COUSCOUS with LAMB & RATATOUILLE

Couscous sounds exotic and therefore presumed difficult to do but it is in fact amazingly simple as all you need to do is put it in a bowl and add hot water!

It can make a good basis for a salad but here the couscous is combined with neck of lamb served with ratatouille which gives the dish a pleasing taste and colour.

INGREDIENTS

Neck of lamb fillets
Couscous
Ratatouille - see recipe on page 118
1 small onion, finely chopped
1 teaspoon of oil
Salt & pepper for seasoning

METHOD

In one pan, cook the ratatouille as per recipe on page 118.
Meanwhile in the second pan, cook the lamb.
Trim off any excess fat and skin from the meat then place in a large heated pan.
Brown the meat on all sides then turn down the heat, cover and cook for 20 minutes.
10 minutes before the end of cooking time, put the couscous in a large bowl and cover with hot water.
Leave for 10 minutes.
When the lamb is cooked, remove the meat and juice from the pan.
Add the oil.
When the oil is hot, add the chopped onions, turn down the heat and cook until soft.
Add the drained couscous and mix well.
Season as necessary then serve with the lamb and ratatouille.

LAMB & COCONUT CURRY

Using the amount of chilli as given, this is a hot curry. However, you can reduce the chilli powder if you prefer it milder. As with all the curries we eat, we serve this with plain boiled rice and add 'small chop' (see page 120).
Coriander naan bread also goes well with this dish.

INGREDIENTS

Plain boiled rice, cooked as per packet instructions

1 teaspoon olive oil
450 gms (1 lbs) lamb, cubed.
1 large onion, chopped
1 teaspoon garlic powder
2 teaspoons ground ginger
2 teaspoons hot chilli powder
1½ teaspoons turmeric
1 tablespoon garam masala
½-1 tin of coconut milk (or 5 oz sachet coconut cream dissolved in 10 fl. oz water)
1 teaspoon salt
⅛ teaspoon black pepper

METHOD

Heat the oil in a large saucepan then add the onions and cook until soft.
Add the garlic, ginger, pepper, turmeric, chilli powder and garam masala and fry for 5 minutes. Add a little water if too dry.
Add the lamb cubes and cook for 5 minutes.
Add the salt and ½ can of coconut milk (or the coconut cream & water) and bring to the boil.
Turn the heat down to low, cover the pan and simmer for ¾ hour or until lamb is tender. Stir the curry from time to time and if using coconut milk, add some more if the sauce becomes too thick.
20 minutes before the end of the cooking time of the curry, use the second pan and cook the rice as per instructions on the packet.
Taste the curry and if necessary bring the flavour up with a little more garam masala.
Drain the rice and serve.

LAMB HOTPOT

If you have a yearning for an old fashioned 'meat and three veg', without the hassle of a full scale roast, try this. The cooking time is over an hour but the dish is easy to prepare and simmers away on a low heat without needing constant attention.

Serve with pan roast potatoes or if you prefer, boiled potatoes.

INGREDIENTS

Potatoes as required

Lamb joint – a half leg or if there are just two of you, try the hocks of lamb which gives each individual his own 'joint' of meat!
1 onion, halved then cut lengthways into thick slices or 8 shallots
4 large carrots – cut into 2" chunks, each chunk cut down the centre then each half cut into three.
225 gms (8 oz) frozen peas.
1 teaspoon garlic powder
½ teaspoon mixed herbs
1 lamb (or vegetable) stock cube
150 ml (¼ pint) of water
1 teaspoon of sugar (sweetener)
1 teaspoon salt
¼ teaspoon ground black pepper

METHOD

Trim off any excess fat on the lamb.
Put a large pan (a wok is ideal if you have a lid for it) on the heat and quickly seal the meat. (Use a little olive oil if you wish.)
Add the onion slices, carrots, garlic, mixed herbs, stock cube, sugar (sweetener), water and pepper.
Bring to the boil, add salt then turn the heat to low, cover and simmer and leave to cook for one hour (depending on size of joint). Just check a couple of times during the cooking to ensure there is sufficient liquid and if necessary add a little water to the pot.
When the meat is cooked, add the peas and taste for seasoning. **Cook** for a further 5 minutes.
Half an hour before the end of the cooking time, start to cook the pot roast potatoes (see recipe on page 115) or boiled potatoes.

You should have a lovely thick gravy at the end of cooking but if it is too thick, add a little water and if too thin, add a little flour (or cornflour) mixed to a liquid paste with water to the gravy, stirring all the time as you add the mixture to ensure it does not go lumpy.

Note

You can of course substitute a piece of pork or beef (brisket is very good cooked this way) for the lamb. The only difference is that with the beef you use a beef stock cube and for the pork, a pork or vegetable stock cube.

MINCED LAMB with PENNE

This is a very simple, quick but attractive dish with the peppers adding a dash of colour.
Serve with a green side salad.

INGREDIENTS

Penne – cooked as per packet instructions

1 teaspoon olive oil
450 gms (1 lb) lean minced lamb
1 onion, finely chopped
1 teaspoon garlic powder
1 red pepper, de-seeded and sliced into strips
1 yellow pepper, de-seeded and sliced into strips
110 gms (4 oz) sliced mushrooms (fresh or tinned)
1 tablespoon plain flour
½ teaspoon mixed herbs
4 tablespoons cream (or 2 generously heaped
tablespoons of (low fat) crème fraîche)
½ teaspoon salt
¼ teaspoon pepper

Garnish (optional)
Parmesan cheese

METHOD

Heat the oil in a saucepan and add the onion, cooking until soft but not brown.
Add the mince and brown.
Add the garlic powder, the pepper strips, sliced mushrooms, herbs, salt & pepper and cook for 25 minutes.
Using the second pan, cook the penne as per packet instructions so that it is ready at the same time as the meat dish.
At the end of cooking time, take the meat pan off the heat and tilt it slightly to allow the juice to gather at one point. Skim off the excess fat.
Sprinkle the flour over the meat, stir in then add the cream (crème fraîche).
Taste and adjust the seasoning as necessary.
Serve on the bed of penne with a side dish of parmesan cheese.

NECK OF LAMB with PASTA

Neck of lamb is a delicious tasting cut of meat and is very suitable for pan cooking. This recipe is a succulent way to cook the lamb and it is both quick & easy to prepare and to cook.

INGREDIENTS

Pasta of choice, cooked as per packet instructions

Neck of lamb fillets
1 teaspoon oil
1 leek, cut lengthways into quarters and then thinly sliced
1 small onion, chopped
100 gms (4 oz) sliced mushrooms (fresh or tinned)
Tin of chopped tomatoes
2 tablespoons tomato puree
1 teaspoon dried mixed herbs
1 teaspoon garlic powder
⅛ teaspoon black pepper
1 teaspoon sugar (or sweetener)
½ teaspoon salt.

METHOD

In one pan, brown the lamb fillets. If you are using non-stick pans, you should not need to add any oil.
Heat the oil in the second pan and add the onions. When soft, add the leeks and cook for a further 2-3 minutes before adding the tomatoes, mushrooms, herbs, garlic, tomato puree, sugar (sweetener), salt and pepper. Stir to mix well.
When the lamb has been browned on all sides, add to the sauce in the first pan.
Bring the mixture to the boil then turn down and simmer with lid on. Cook for 15 minutes.
Meanwhile, wash out the first pan in readiness to cook the pasta.
After the lamb has been cooking for 15 minutes, cook the pasta as per the instructions on the packet.
When the pasta is cooked, drain and taste the lamb sauce for seasoning. Adjust if necessary and serve.

PASTA WITH PORK and PEPPERS

You can choose what type of pasta you want for this quick, subtle flavoured dish but we use penne.

INGREDIENTS

Pasta of choice, cooked as per instructions on packet.

2 tablespoons soy sauce
½ tablespoon olive oil
1 teaspoon sugar (sweetener)
1 teaspoon ground ginger
1 teaspoon garlic granules
450 gms (1 lb) pork fillet
1 small onion, finely sliced
1 red pepper, finely sliced
1 green pepper, finely sliced
60 ml (2 fl. oz) single cream or 1 generous tablespoon of (low fat) crème fraîche
½ teaspoon salt
¼ teaspoon ground black pepper

Garnish
Chopped parsley (optional)

METHOD

In a bowl, mix together the soy sauce, olive oil, sugar (sweetener), garlic and ginger.
Trim the pork fillet of any excess fat and sinew then cut into thin strips. Add the pork to the marinade, tossing the pork well to ensure all the strips are coated with the marinade. Leave for at least 30 minutes.
When ready to cook, heat a saucepan then add the pork mixture and quickly brown. Remove the meat from the saucepan.
Add the peppers and the onion to the pan. Cook gently until the onion is soft then return the pork to the pan together with the salt and pepper. Re-heat and then turn the heat to low, cover and simmer for 20 minutes.
At this point put the pan of water on for the pasta and cook as per packet instructions.

When the pasta is ready, quickly add the cream (crème fraîche) to the pork mixture and stir in well. Taste and adjust seasoning as required.
Drain the pasta and place in serving bowl or individual bowls, take the pork mixture off the heat and portion out on top of the pasta.
Sprinkle chopped parsley over the top (optional) and serve.

PIQUANT PORK

This is one of our favourite dishes, the sauce having a wonderful B-B-Q flavour due to the Worcester sauce, mustard, tomato and sugar combination.

As with all our recipes that have sugar, we substitute sweetener for the real thing – works a treat.

INGREDIENTS

Plain boiled rice, cooked as per packet instructions
225 gms (8 oz) frozen peas

1 teaspoon olive oil
450 gms (1 lb) sparerib pork chops
½ teaspoon garlic powder
1 onion, chopped
150 gms (5 oz) tomato puree
½ teaspoon salt
¼ teaspoon pepper
½ teaspoon mixed herbs
4 tablespoons brown sugar (2 - 4 teaspoons sweetener)
4 tablespoons Worcester sauce
½ beef stock cube
125 ml (4 fl. oz) water
2 teaspoons mustard

METHOD

Heat the oil in a large saucepan then add the onions. Cook gently until soft.
Add the garlic, tomato puree, salt, pepper, herbs, sugar (or sweetener), Worcester sauce, stock cube, water and mustard. Mix well and cook for 5 minutes whilst preparing the meat.
De-bone and trim excess fat off the spareribs and cut into bite size cubes. Add to pan, stir to cover the pork with the sauce and bring to the boil.
Immediately turn down the heat, cover and simmer for 40/45 minutes.
In the meantime, using the second pan, cook the rice so that it is ready at the same time as the meat dish, adding the peas to the rice 5 minutes from the end of the cooking time.
When all is ready, taste the pork dish for seasoning and sweetness.
Serve.

PORK with COURGETTE PASTA

This dish of pork and mushrooms is lifted out of the ordinary when served with pasta tossed with courgettes and parmesan cheese.
Any short pasta such as fusilli, farfalle, conchiglie or penne can be used.

INGREDIENTS

Short pasta of choice - cooked as per packet instructions
2 large courgettes, washed, sliced lengthways four ways
then cut into ½" thick wedges
3 tablespoons parmesan cheese

1 teaspoon of olive oil
450 gms (1lb) lean pork fillet, cut into small thin slices
1 small onion, halved and sliced
3 tablespoons tomato puree
110 gms (4 oz) fresh or small tin of sliced or button mushrooms
1 chicken stock cube
1 teaspoon garlic powder
1 teaspoon mixed herbs
150 ml (5 fl oz) water
1 teaspoon sugar (sweetener)
1 teaspoon of Worcester Sauce
½ teaspoon salt
¼ teaspoon black pepper

METHOD

Heat 2 teaspoons of oil in a large pan/wok then on medium heat add the courgettes, cooking for approximately 15 minutes until tender and turning frequently to get all sides golden brown.
Meanwhile in the second pan, heat the oil over a moderate heat then add the onions and cook until soft.
Add the pork to brown then the stock cube, water, tomato puree, herbs, garlic, Worcester sauce, salt, pepper and sugar (sweetener).
Mix well, bring to the boil then lower the heat to simmer, cover and cook for 15 minutes before adding the mushrooms. Continue cooking.
When the courgettes are ready, remove from the heat and keep warm (I put them in a bowl and pop another bowl on top).
Wash the pan out and cook the pasta.
When the pasta is cooked, drain then add the courgettes and 2 tablespoons of parmesan cheese to the pasta. Mix well and just before serving sprinkle the remaining tablespoon of cheese on top.
Check the pork dish for seasoning and serve.

PORK IN MUSHROOM CREAM SAUCE with PASTA

This is a quick and delicate flavoured dish that goes well with any pasta - long strands such as spaghetti or tagliatelle or short such as penne or macaroni – choose whichever you have to hand.

INGREDIENTS

Pasta of choice cooked as per instructions on packet but with a vegetable stock cube added to the water.

450 gms (1 lb) fillet of pork
1 onion, finely chopped
1 tablespoon + 1 teaspoon olive oil
⅛ teaspoon ground black pepper
½ teaspoon mixed herbs
1 teaspoon garlic powder
110 gms (4 oz) sliced mushrooms (fresh or tinned)
¼ teaspoon paprika
150 ml (5 fl. oz) single cream (or 2 generous tablespoons of (low fat) crème fraîche)
½ teaspoon mustard
Salt to taste

Garnish
Freshly chopped parsley

METHOD

In a bowl mix the tablespoon of olive oil, the pepper, garlic powder and the mixed herbs. (I use a small plastic pot with lid which allows me to shake up the marinade from time to time.)
Cut the pork fillet into thin strips then add to the marinade for 30 minutes. Make sure the pork is evenly coated with the marinade.
Heat the remaining teaspoon of oil in a large saucepan, add the chopped onion and cook until soft but not brown.
In the second pan, start to cook the pasta.
Add the pork to the onions and cook for 10 minutes before adding the sliced mushrooms.
Cook for a further 5 minutes.
Add the cream (crème fraîche), paprika and the mustard. Add salt to taste and cook until the sauce has reduced and thickened.
Serve on the bed of pasta and sprinkle freshly chopped parsley over the top.

SOY PORK

This dish originally used tagliatelle but any pasta will do and unless we are able to buy fresh tagliatelle we substitute penne. Again, if eating outdoors on laps the short pasta might be easier to handle!

INGREDIENTS

Pasta of choice cooked as per instructions on the packet.

1 teaspoon olive oil
1 large onion
1 green pepper
450 gms (1 lb) pork fillet
75 gms (3 oz) sliced mushrooms (fresh or tinned)
2 tablespoons soy sauce
1 tablespoon tomato puree
1 tablespoon brown sugar (2 teaspoons sweetener)
125 ml (4 fl oz) water
1 teaspoon garlic granules
Salt and pepper to season.

Garnish (optional)
Chopped parsley

METHOD

Thinly slice the pork, onions, pepper and mushrooms if using fresh.
Heat the oil then add the onions and pepper. Cook until the onion is soft.
Add the pork and garlic and cook for a further 10 minutes.
Add the mushrooms and cook for a further 5 minutes.
Stir in the soy sauce, tomato puree, sugar (sweetener) and water.
Bring to the boil then lower the heat to simmer, cover and cook for 15 minutes.
Now using the second pan, cook the pasta.
When ready, taste the pork mixture and if necessary, add salt and pepper. However be cautious. Soy sauce has salt in it and I do not normally need to add any seasoning at all.
Drain the cooked pasta, add the pork mixture and combine well.
Sprinkle the chopped parsley over the top and serve.

PAELLA

This is a wonderful, ONE pan meal. I use my wok for this and you should use the largest, flat bottomed pan you have to hand.
If you like pepperoni sausage, add some to the dish at the same time as the peas and seafood. On the Continent, many paella recipes contain 2 meats (such as chicken and rabbit or lamb) and 2 fish (such as prawns and mussels).
Also, if you do have the luxury of an oven/microwave, Garlic bread goes very well with this dish!

INGREDIENTS

1 teaspoon olive oil
8 pieces of chicken or packet of chicken thighs, skinned, boned then cut it into large chunks
Packet of seafood mix (frozen or fresh)
225 gms (8 oz) prawns (frozen or fresh)
1 medium onion, chopped
Large can chopped tomatoes
1 large red pepper, de-seeded and chopped into strips
225 gms (8 oz) rice
225 ml (8 fl oz) water
225 gms (8 oz) frozen peas
½ teaspoon lemon juice
1 teaspoon salt
½ teaspoon pepper
1 teaspoon paprika
1 teaspoon garlic granules
1 teaspoon turmeric

Garnish (optional)
Freshly chopped parsley
Slices of hard boiled egg

METHOD

Heat the oil in the wok/pan.
Add the chicken pieces and cook for 10/15 minutes. Remove and keep hot.
Add the onions to the pan and cook 5/7 minutes until soft but not brown then add the tomatoes, red pepper, salt, pepper, paprika and garlic and cook 5 minutes.
Add the rice to the pan and mix well, frying for 3 minutes until the rice is transparent.
Now add the water, lemon juice and turmeric.

Bring the mixture up to the boil, return the chicken to the pan then lower the heat to simmer.
Cook for 15 minutes, stirring occasionally to check if more water is required.
Add the seafood mixture, prawns and peas and cook for a further 10 minutes or until chicken and rice are cooked and the liquid has been absorbed.
Transfer the paella to a serving dish and garnish with slices of hard boiled egg and chopped parsley.
Serve.

NOTE
If you have any paella left over, save it and use it as a filling for an omelette.
Make up and cook the omelette as normal and when ready, just before flipping over one half, spread the (gently) reheated paella over the omelette.
Serve with a salad and crusty bread.

PRAWN & RICE SALAD

This salad can be eaten on its own with fresh bread of choice for a light lunch/supper or can form part of a larger salad meal. It's also a very tasty way of using up left over rice.
If you prefer, ham can be substituted for the prawns.

INGREDIENTS

(Approx.) 175 gms (6 oz) cooked plain boiled rice
(if cooking the rice at the time, rinse in cold water immediately after cooking)
2 tomatoes, de-seeded and cut into small pieces
Tin of cut green beans
3/4 tablespoons of (light) mayonnaise
450 gms (1 lb) cooked and peeled prawns
1 teaspoon garlic powder (optional)
½ teaspoon salt
¼ teaspoon pepper.
Garlic powder (optional)

METHOD

Place the cooked rice in a bowl and mix with 3 tablespoons of mayonnaise. All the rice should be coated with mayonnaise so if necessary add another tablespoon of mayonnaise.
Now add the salt, pepper and garlic (if using) and mix again.
Add the chopped tomatoes, green beans and prawns and toss well.
Taste and adjust seasoning as required.
Serve immediately or cover and leave in the fridge until required.

PRAWN CURRY 1

A very simple dish to prepare that has a very light flavour and certainly should not to be confused with a heavy vindaloo! Even those who think they don't like curry should try this one.

INGREDIENTS

Plain boiled rice cooked as per packet instructions

1 teaspoon olive oil
I large onion, cut in half and thinly sliced
1 teaspoon garlic powder
1 tablespoon curry powder
1 teaspoon lemon concentrate or 2 teaspoons fresh lemon juice
2 tablespoon tomato puree
300 ml (10 fl. oz) water
1 fish cube
50 gms (2 oz) sultanas
450 gms (1 lb) fresh or frozen cooked, shelled prawns

Garnish (optional)
De-seeded and chopped tomato
Sliced fresh banana
Chopped hard boiled egg

METHOD

In one pan, cook the rice as per the packet instructions.
In the second pan, heat the oil and fry the onions until soft and lightly brown.
Add the curry powder, garlic, lemon, tomato puree, fish cube, water and sultanas. Cook for 5 minutes.
Add the prawns and cook further 5 minutes then taste for seasoning.
Serve, garnished with de-seeded chopped tomatoes, sliced fresh banana and chopped boiled egg.

Note
If you have any of this or indeed any other curry left over, re-heat it the following day and use as a filling in pita bread with salad.

PRAWN CURRY 2

This is another very easy curry but it is hotter than prawn curry 1. **Serve** with naan bread, plain boiled rice and of course 'small chop'!

INGREDIENTS

Plain boiled rice, cooked as per packet instructions

1 teaspoon olive oil
1 onion finely chopped
1 teaspoon of garlic powder
450 gms (1 lb) cooking prawns
1½ teaspoons garam masala powder
1 teaspoon chilli powder
½ teaspoon ground turmeric
Salt and pepper to taste
1 teaspoon flour/cornflour
90 ml (3 fl. oz) water

Garnish (optional)
De-seeded and chopped tomato
Sliced banana
Hard boiled egg, chopped

METHOD

In one pan, cook the rice as per instructions on the packet.
In the second pan, heat the oil in a large saucepan then add the onion and cook for 3-4 minutes until soft but not brown.
Add prawns and fry for further 1-2 minutes.
Add the garam masala, chilli powder, turmeric and garlic then cook for further minute, stirring well.
Mix the cornflour/flour with the water and stirring constantly, add to the pan.
Season with salt & pepper, cover the pan and cook gently for 10-15 minutes until the liquid has thickened.
Serve on a bed of rice and sprinkle over the garnish if required.

SMOKED MACKEREL KEDGEREE

Although smoked haddock is the usual fish in kedgeree, we enjoy the smoked mackerel that you can buy in vacuum packs at most supermarkets. It's a lot easier to obtain and keeps well in the fridge until required. Give it a go. It's quick, simple to make and as 'oily' fish, it's also good for you!

INGREDIENTS

175 gms (6 oz) of rice
350 gms (12 oz) smoked mackerel
2 hard boiled eggs
1 small, chopped onion
Salt & Pepper to taste
Teaspoon of olive oil

Garnish (optional)
Chopped parsley (fresh)
1 de-seeded and chopped tomato

METHOD

Bring a pan of water to boil and cook the rice in the normal way.
Take out any remaining bones in the fish, peel off the skin and place in a large saucepan of boiling water.
Turn off the heat and leave the fish to stand in the water for 5 minutes.
Drain the fish and flake into pieces.
Wipe the saucepan clean then heat the teaspoon of oil and add the chopped onions. Cook gently until soft but not brown.
Whilst waiting for the rice and onions to cook, shell and dice up one of the hard boiled eggs. (If you do not already have some hard boiled eggs to hand, cook the two eggs [making sure their shells are wiped clean] with the rice.)
Once the rice is cooked, drain well and add to the onions together with the fish and chopped egg. Add the chopped tomato if required.
Mix well and season to taste. Turn heat down to the lowest possible setting and leave to warm through – 5/10 minutes.
Serve garnished with the slices or wedges of hard boiled egg and chopped parsley.

TUNA STEAK with PRAWN SAUCE

On holiday in Portugal a few years ago, my husband ordered a steak. The steak was served with a beautiful seafood mix sauce and this recipe is a variation on that combination.

The tuna can be served either with pasta or potatoes and a green vegetable such as peas or green beans.

INGREDIENTS

Potatoes/greens or Pasta of choice

Fresh Tuna Steaks
225 grams (8 oz) cooked prawns
1 teaspoon garlic powder
½ teaspoon salt + pinch of salt and pepper
2 tablespoons flour
25 gms (1 oz) butter or spread suitable for cooking
300 ml (10 fl. oz milk) full, semi or skimmed

METHOD

In one pan, melt the butter/spread then taking the pan off the heat add the flour with a little milk and beat to form a paste.
Gradually add half the milk then gently re-heat, stirring all the time until the sauce thickens. Add the remaining milk and again stirring all the time, bring to the boil.
Stir in the pinch of salt and pepper then set the sauce aside (I use a small plastic pot with lid).
Wash the pan out and cook the potatoes or pasta as normal. If you are including vegetables, add these to the pan 5/8 minutes before the end of cooking time depending on the vegetable being used.
12 minutes before the end of the cooking time of the potatoes or pasta, heat up a flat bottom pan/wok with a teaspoon of oil.
Sprinkle one side of the tuna with garlic powder then place the steak in the pan garlic side down and cook for 2 minutes.
Sprinkle more garlic on the top side of the tuna steak then flip the steak over and cook for a further 5 minutes.
Turn the steak over once more and cook for a further 5 minutes or until the steak is cooked through.
Remove the tuna steaks and quickly re-heat the white sauce in the pan incorporating any juice from the tuna steaks.
Add the prawns and when fully heated through, (2/3 minutes) pour the sauce over the tuna steaks and serve.

POTATO & ONION OMELETTE

Very quick and easy, this omelette is a meal in itself and can be served with a side salad and/or fresh bread.
Additional fillings can be added, such as ham, peas, tomatoes but try the original recipe first!

INGREDIENTS

3 large/4 medium sized eggs
Small tin of new potatoes
1 onion, finely chopped
Pinch of salt and pepper for seasoning
2 tablespoons cold water
1 teaspoon of olive oil

METHOD

Drain the tin of potatoes and thinly slice the potatoes.
Heat the oil in a large flat bottom pan/wok then add the onions. On medium to low heat, fry the onions until soft then add the potato slices and continue cooking, moving the mixture about to avoid sticking, until potatoes are heated through and beginning to brown.
Break the eggs into mixing bowl/jug and lightly beat. Add the salt and pepper to season and the water. Lightly re-mix.
On medium heat, pour the liquid onto the potatoes & onions. After 3-4 minutes, lift the sides of the omelette to allow the raw liquid resting on top to reach the bottom.
Continue to cook until the egg mixture is solid. (If you have the luxury of a grill, once the top is almost solid, take off the heat and finish the dish off under the grill until it is golden brown.)
Serve either in wedges or fold over half the omelette (to make a traditional omelette shape), cut in two and serve.

STUFFED EGGS

These hard boiled eggs, stuffed with sardines, make a delightful starter to a meal or can form part of a larger salad or be simply served as they are, with or without salad and fresh bread.
Easy to prepare they can be made in advance and kept in the fridge until required.

INGREDIENTS

6 hard boiled eggs
1 tin sardines in brine
1-2 tablespoons (light) mayonnaise
Salt and pepper for seasoning

Garnish (optional)
Finely chopped parsley
Tomato wedges

METHOD

Shell the hard boiled eggs and cut in two – length ways.
Scoop out the yolk and place in bowl. Set the whites aside for filling later.
Drain the sardines, split down the centre and take out the spine and innards then add the sardines to the egg yolks.
Mash the egg yolks and sardines together with a little mayonnaise. (I use the 'light' reduced fat kind) until the mixture is smooth.
Season with salt and pepper to taste.
Spoon the mixture back into the half egg whites. Use all of the egg & sardine mixture, piling the mixture on top of the whites as well as in the 'well'. Sprinkle the tops with chopped parsley.
Place in fridge until required.
If serving as a starter, place some chopped lettuce on a serving plate and arrange the half eggs on top. Cut a tomato into segments and place a wedge between each half egg.

BANANA FLAN

In the 25 years that I have been making this desert, I have come across quite a few similar recipes but they all seem to require additional sugar and butter on top of the already sweetened can of condensed milk.
Originally I used to make the caramel filling by boiling the unopened can of condensed milk for 3 hours although the manufacturers now warn against this and today you can buy a tin of pre-made caramel. This makes an already easy dish even easier and with only four ingredients that require just putting together it is a perfect dish for caravanning - or for those who don't like to cook!
This desert is best with ripe bananas and the flavour is enhanced by leaving overnight. It also freezes well (although in my experience, left overs are very rare!)

INGREDIENTS

Large sponge flan case (you can of course make this but
especially whilst in the camper I buy the pre-made ones)
1 tin caramel
2/3 ripe bananas
300 ml. (10 fl. oz) double cream
Half walnuts to decorate

METHOD

Place the flan on a serving dish
Slice the bananas and spread over the base of the flan so that it is well covered.
Open the tin of caramel and using a spatula, spread the filling over the bananas making sure all the banana slices are covered. To aid the spreading, dip the spatula from time to time into a jug or pan of hot water – imagine you are spreading icing over a cake. You may start off thinking that there is not enough filling to cover the bananas but work methodically and the mixture will fill the flan case to the top!
If you are keeping the flan overnight before eating, put the flan into the fridge, otherwise beat the cream until it forms soft peaks then spread over the flan.
Finally, decorate with half walnuts (or any other decoration of your choice such as chocolate chips).
If eating the flan later, remove the flan from the fridge at least half an hour before eating to allow the flan to reach room temperature then whip up the cream, spread over the flan and decorate as above.

CHOCOLATE POTS
with PINEAPPLE

This looks (and tastes!) like a very rich, elaborate desert but is in fact very simple to put together. The original recipe comes from Belgium where it is one of their national dishes.

INGREDIENTS

Box of chocolate cups
Small tin of pineapple chunks/rings in natural juices
300 ml (10 oz) double cream
2 tablespoons sherry
½ packet of trifle sponges

METHOD

Place the chocolate cups on a serving plate.
Break up the trifle sponges and put one piece in the bottom of each cup.
Drain the pineapple but reserve some of the juice. Cut the pineapple into small wedges and place 4-6 pieces around and over the sponge.
Now mix the sherry with 2 tablespoons of the reserved pineapple juice and dribble this over the sponge pieces.
Whip the cream until it makes soft peaks. Spoon the cream over the pineapple and trifle sponges until it fully fills the cup.
Decorate on top with 2-3 additional pieces of pineapple.

NOTE

If you want to really impress, make your own chocolate pots! This is quite time consuming but is a good alternative if you find dark chocolate too bitter as you can buy a milk chocolate bar - but buy the chocolate with the highest percentage of cocoa solids. Break the chocolate into pieces in a bowl placed over a saucepan full of hot water. Slowly melt the chocolate. Now using paper baking cups, take a clean pastry brush and 'paint' on a thin layer of chocolate over the paper cup. Leave the chocolate to set then 'paint ' a second layer and if necessary a third. Place in fridge and allow to completely harden before peeling off the paper wrapping. This has to be done with great care as the chocolate cups are quite delicate.

COFFEE and WHISKEY TRIFLE

This trifle uses cream, whiskey and coffee essence to make a delectable, rich dessert for special occasions. Nevertheless, it is easy to prepare and will impress wherever you are entertaining!

INGREDIENTS

1 packet of trifle sponges
2 tablespoons coffee essence
4 tablespoons whiskey
75 gms (3 oz) castor sugar (3 tablespoons sweetener)
75 gms (3 oz) cornflour (3 level tablespoons)
600 ml (1 pint) milk (full, semi or skimmed)
2 egg yolks
300 ml (10 fl. oz) double cream
Half walnuts for decoration

METHOD

Break up trifle sponges into the bottom of a suitable bowl.
Mix half the coffee essence with 3 tablespoons of the whiskey and dribble over the sponges, coating the sponges as evenly as possible.
Next put the cornflour into a small saucepan and add the milk, a little at a time to blend with the cornflour then add the sugar and heat up, stirring continuously until the sauce thickens and boils. If you are using sweetener, put 2 tablespoons in the custard and taste before adding more sweetener if necessary. Cook gently for a further 3 minutes.
Remove the pan from the heat and stir in the egg yolks and remaining coffee essence. Return to the heat and cook for a further minute. Remove again from the heat and stir in the remaining whiskey then allow the custard to cool.
When the custard has cooled, whip the cream until it forms soft peaks. Fold half of the cream into the custard and then spoon the custard over the sponges.
Spread the remaining cream over the trifle and decorate on top with walnuts.

FRESH FRUIT SALAD

There is nothing quite so refreshing as a bowl of fresh fruit salad, served on its own at breakfast or with ice-cream &/or cream for desert and yet it is so simple to make.

The recipe given here uses the left over mango, paw-paw (papaya) and pineapple from a curry but any fruit in season can be added to the bowl.

INGREDIENTS

1-2 tablespoon sugar (sweetener)
300 ml (10 fl. oz) water
1 teaspoon of concentrated or 2 teaspoons fresh lemon juice
Fresh fruit of choice

As shown in photograph:
Mango - peeled and cut into cubes
Paw-paw (papaya), de-seeded, skinned and chopped into cubes
Pineapple (fresh or tinned) cut into cubes
1-2 bananas, sliced
2 red desert apples, chopped with skin left on
Strawberries - cut in half

Other fruit that can be used:
Oranges - peeled and segmented
Grapes- red or white
Kiwi fruit- peeled and sliced
Plums, halved or quartered depending on size
Raspberries
Cherries
Melon - cut into cubes

METHOD

Heat the water and sugar together until the sugar has dissolved. (You can also add 2 tablespoons of liqueur or sherry if you wish!) Taste for personal sweetness.
Add the lemon juice (which helps to keep the fruit from discolouring).
Allow the water to cool and transfer to large bowl.
Add the prepared chopped fruit and stir well to ensure all the fruit gets a coating of the juice.
Cover with an air tight lid or cling film and let the fruit infuse until required.

FRIED BANANAS

Bananas quickly fried in a little oil makes a delicious dessert served with either cream or ice-cream. However they can also make an interesting accompaniment to savoury dishes.

METHOD

Heat a flat bottom pan or wok with a teaspoon of oil (you may require more oil if you are not using a non stick pan).
Peel and slice the bananas lengthwise then place flat side down in the pan.
On medium heat, cook the bananas for a couple of minutes until they are warmed through and turning light brown.
Using a fish spatula gently turn the bananas over and cook for a further 2 minutes.
Serve.

RICE PUDDING

If you like the brown skin of an oven cooked rice pudding, you might be disappointed with this version for, cooked on top in a saucepan, it has no skin at all. It is, however, a deliciously creamy rice pudding which has the added bonus of taking under 30 minutes to cook.
Try it!

INGREDIENTS

4 rounded tablespoons of pudding (or ordinary savoury) rice
600 ml (1 pint) full, semi skimmed or skimmed milk
Sugar (sweetener) to taste
1 egg

METHOD

Put the rice in a sieve and rinse well in cold water.
Put the rice into a saucepan with the milk. Stir well to avoid the rice sticking to the bottom and bring to the boil. Stir again, lower the heat to simmer, cover and cook for 20 minutes – or until the rice is soft.
Take the pan off the heat and add sugar to taste – this is usually 2 tablespoons but can be adjusted to your own requirements. Start with one tablespoon and work up!
Lightly beat the egg then quickly incorporate into the rice.
Return the pan to the heat and bring back up to boil. This should make the rice pudding a lovely creamy consistency but if it is too liquid, cook for a further few minutes to evaporate some of the liquid (or add an extra egg). If the mixture has gone too thick, add a little extra milk to the required consistency.

Cream of VEGETABLE SOUP

As full timers in our camper van, we enjoy a meal of soup and bread on the colder days.

I must admit I do miss my blender when it comes to sieving the vegetables but I still consider the effort worth it!

INGREDIENTS

1 large onion) Try a bag of mixed
3 carrots) vegetables for stews
1 leek)
Swede (optional))
½ green cabbage or 2 courgettes
2 potatoes
110 gms (4 oz) peas (fresh or frozen)
Fresh or tin of green beans
2 vegetable stock cubes
1¼ litre (2 pints) water
150 ml (5 fl. oz) milk
2 teaspoons mixed herbs
1-2 teaspoons salt
½ -1 teaspoon pepper

Garnish
Chopped parsley (optional)

METHOD

Put the water and stock cubes in a large saucepan and begin to bring to the boil.
Finely chop the onion and leek and add to the water.
Peel and cut the swede and carrots into small chunks. Peel and similarly chop the potatoes and add to the pan.
Thinly slice the cabbage or cut the courgettes lengthways into quarters then chop into small pieces.
Add to the pan, followed by the peas, green beans, mixed herbs, 1 teaspoon of the salt and ½ teaspoon pepper.
When the water has come to the boil, turn the heat down, cover and simmer for 45 minutes until the vegetables have thoroughly cooked.
Work the vegetables through a sieve (or blender) and return the soup to the pan. Re-heat the soup, adding the milk.
Taste and add more salt and pepper if necessary.
Sprinkle chopped parsley over the top of the soup before serving.

FRUIT STARTERS

AVOCADOS
with Worcester Sauce

METHOD

Wash the avocados then cut lengthways in two.
Remove the stone (chop your knife blade into the stone and making sure it has a good purchase, carefully wriggle the stone loose).
At time of serving, pour a generous amount of Worcester Sauce into the centre well.
Serve.

MANGO HEDGEHOGS

METHOD

1. With a sharp knife, cut down the length of the mango, roughly ½" to each side of the stalk. Discard the centre which has the large stone in it.

2. Cut strips down the length of each half of the mango being careful not to cut down into the skin.

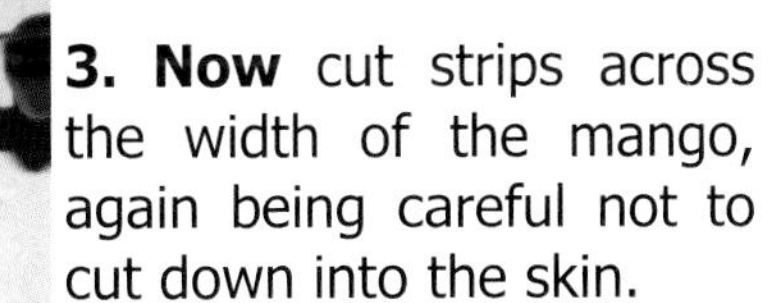

3. Now cut strips across the width of the mango, again being careful not to cut down into the skin.

4. Carefully invert the mango to make a dome so that the flesh splits at the cuts and forms separate chunks. **Serve.**

PAW PAW WITH LEMON (Papaya)

METHOD

Cut the paw paw (papaya) lengthways down the centre.
Scoop out the black seeds.
Sprinkle the halves of the fruit with lemon juice.
Serve.

Note

Both the paw paw above and the mango hedgehogs make a wonderful fruit to eat at breakfast too.

MACARONI CHEESE with.......

Most people know about macaroni cheese. It is a tasty and quick meal, especially if served with the addition of diced ham and/or with some fresh crusty bread and side salad but it also makes a great accompaniment to pan fried meat or sausages.

INGREDIENTS

Macaroni - or any short pasta of choice - cooked as per instructions on packet

Sauce:
25 gms (1oz) butter or spread suitable for cooking
2 tablespoons plain flour
300 ml (10 fl. oz) milk (full,semi or skimmed)
110 gms (4 oz) grated cheddar cheese
Pinch of pepper

METHOD

Make the sauce whilst the pasta is cooking in the first pan.
Melt the butter/spread in the second pan then take off the heat, stir in the flour and a little of the milk and beat to form a paste.
Add approximately half the milk then gently heat, stirring all the time until the sauce thickens. Add the remaining milk and again, stirring all the time, bring to the boil.
Add the pinch of pepper and the cheese to the pan and continue to stir until the cheese has melted.
Taste and if necessary add a little salt and if the sauce has become too thick, add a little more milk.
When the pasta is just cooked, drain and add to the cheese sauce, mixing well to ensure all the pasta is coated with the sauce.
Serve on its own or with added ham or pan fried meat or sausages (the macaroni can be kept warm with the lid on whilst you cook the meat in the washed out first pan).

MINESTRONE SOUP

This soup makes a very good starter for a formal meal but is also a meal in itself served with fresh bread of your choice. Put a bowl of grated parmesan cheese on the table and liberally sprinkle the cheese over the soup at the time of eating.

If you want to keep the soup vegetarian, substitute the chicken stock cubes with vegetable ones and omit the bacon.

INGREDIENTS

1 teaspoon olive oil
50 gms (2 oz) bacon, finely chopped
1 medium sized onion, finely chopped
2 celery stalks, finely chopped
175 gms (6 oz) carrots, finely chopped (2 large carrots)
2 tomatoes, chopped
1 teaspoon garlic powder
225 gms (8 oz) leeks, finely chopped (1 leek)
175 gms (6 oz) courgettes, finely chopped
1½ litres (2½ pints) water
2 chicken stock cubes
½ teaspoon mixed herbs
75 gms (3 oz) macaroni (or other suitable pasta such as farfallini)
1 tablespoon tomato puree
1 teaspoon salt
½ teaspoon ground black pepper

Garnish (optional)
Chopped parsley
Parmesan cheese

METHOD

Heat the oil in a large saucepan and add the bacon. Cook for 2 minutes then add the onions, celery, carrots and tomatoes.
Lower the heat to minimum, cover and sweat the vegetables for 15 minutes stirring occasionally to avoid the vegetables sticking.
Add the garlic, salt, pepper, herbs, water & stock cubes, bring to the boil then lower the heat, recover the pan and simmer for 30 minutes.
Add the leeks, courgettes & pasta and cook for a further 25 minutes.
Finally stir in the tomato puree and cook for further 5 minutes.
Sprinkle the chopped parsley over the soup just before serving.
Having served the soup in individual bowls, don't forget to sprinkle the parmesan cheese on top!

MUSHROOM STROGANOFF

This quick, light meal is served with rice but can just as easily become a tasty sauce for pasta.

INGREDIENTS

Boiled rice cooked as per packet instructions

1 teaspoon oil
1 onion, finely chopped
250 gms (10 oz) mushrooms (closed cup), wiped and sliced
1 teaspoon mustard
½ tablespoon tomato puree
1 teaspoon garlic powder
½ teaspoon paprika
⅛ teaspoon black pepper
½ teaspoon salt
90 ml (3 fl. oz) water
2 tablespoons of (low fat) crème fraîche

METHOD

In one pan, cook the rice as per packet instructions.
In the second pan, heat the oil then add the onions, turn down the heat and cook until soft.
Add the mustard, tomato puree, garlic powder, paprika, salt and pepper. Mix well then add the water.
Add the mushrooms and bring to the boil.
Turn down the heat, cover and simmer for 15 minutes.
Add the cream (crème fraîche) to the mushroom sauce. If the mixture is a little too liquid, add a little flour paste (flour or cornflour mixed with cold water) until you reach the required consistency.
Taste for seasoning.
Serve.

PAN ROAST POTATOES

If you thought you could not have roast potatoes without an oven, think again! These roast potatoes are done on the top of the stove and use very little oil. Nevertheless they are crispy on the outside and fluffy light on the inside.

METHOD

Peel the required amount of potatoes and halve or quarter depending on size.
Place in a pan of cold water and bring to the boil.
Add a little salt and part cook the potatoes for 15 minutes.
Drain into a sieve.
In a large flat bottom pan/wok, heat 2 teaspoons of oil and one teaspoon of butter (or cooking spread) together.
Quickly shake the potatoes about in the sieve to scuff the outside and then place in the hot pan.
Lower the heat to medium and cook the potatoes, turning to brown all sides which should be golden and crisp by the time the potatoes are fully cooked. They should be done within 15 minutes.
Add a little more oil if it becomes necessary, especially if you are not using a non stick pan.

PARSLEY TOMATOES

These tomatoes make a wonderful side dish that goes with virtually any meat or fish dish but particularly with chops or pasta dishes such as lasagne. They can also form part of a salad table.

INGREDIENTS

4 ripe beef tomatoes (or if not available, 8 large salad tomatoes)
½ onion, very finely chopped
large bunch of fresh parsley, very finely chopped
2-4 tablespoons olive oil
1-2 tablespoon vinegar
¼ teaspoon salt
¼ teaspoon pepper

METHOD

In a bowl, combine the olive oil, vinegar, salt and pepper. Add the finely chopped onion and parsley and mix well.
Thickly slice the tomatoes.
Arrange a layer of tomatoes on a serving plate and place a heaped teaspoon of the onion/parsley mixture in the centre of each slice of tomato. If there are still some slices of tomato left over, arrange these as a second layer and again put a heaped teaspoon of the onion/parsley mixture on each slice.
Use up all of the onion/parsley mixture including the oil/vinegar dressing.
Serve when ready but try and allow at least ½ hour 'resting' to allow the separate flavours to blend.

RATATOUILLE

Ratatouille is a wonderful mixture of Mediterranean vegetables cooked together to form a rich and colourful accompaniment to meat - especially lamb. It does, however, also make a very tasty sauce for pasta.

INGREDIENTS

1 aubergine, cut into small cubes
2 medium sized courgettes, cut into small cubes
1 onion, finely chopped
1 leek, quartered lengthways then thinly sliced
1 pepper (yellow) chopped
1 tin chopped tomatoes
2 tablespoons tomato puree
½ teaspoon mixed herbs
2 teaspoons sugar (sweetener)
½ teaspoon salt
¼ teaspoon pepper

METHOD

Put all the ingredients, except the tomato puree, into a pan and bring to the boil.
Stir the ingredients well, lower the heat to simmer, cover with a lid and cook for 30 minutes or until the vegetables have cooked down.
Stir in the tomato puree and taste for seasoning.
Serve.

SMALL CHOP
for Curries

Top row: banana, desiccated coconut, paw-paw. 2nd row: mango pickle, chopped egg, sultanas. Bottom row: mango, tomato & raw onion, pineapple.

My husband grew up in Kenya and there they accompanied curries with bowls of what they called 'small chop' - dishes of de-seeded chopped tomatoes, chopped boiled eggs, desiccated coconut, chopped paw-paw (papaya), finely chopped raw onions, pineapple chunks, slices of banana, mango, chutneys and sultanas.

If you have never tried these with curries please do - if not the whole range, definitely the chopped tomatoes with raw onions and bananas. You'll never look back!

If you don't use all the mango, paw-paw, pineapple or banana with the curry, use them as the basis for a fruit salad (see recipe, page 99)

STUFFED TOMATOES

Stuffed with prawns in mayonnaise, these tomatoes can be eaten as a starter to a formal dinner or can form part of a larger salad or simply served on their own with some fresh bread of choice, as a light lunch/supper.

Any way you eat them, they are simply delicious!

INGREDIENTS

4 ripe beef tomatoes (if beef tomatoes are not available you
can use large salad tomatoes but allow 2 per person)
450 gms (1 lb) of cooked, peeled prawns
3-4 tablespoons of (light) mayonnaise
1 teaspoon garlic powder
Salt to taste

Garnish
Sprigs of parsley

METHOD

Wash the tomatoes then slice off (but retain) the top ½" of the tomatoes.
Scoop out and discard the centre seeds and core. (Taking a sharp kitchen knife, cut around the centre, cut diagonally four ways and scoop out.) Lightly sprinkle some salt into the tomato shells.
Put the prawns into a sieve and rinse under cold water. Drain well and pat dry with kitchen towel then put into a bowl.
Add the garlic powder and spoon on 3 tablespoons of mayonnaise.
Mix well.
Taste and add a little salt and some more mayonnaise if required.
Spoon the mixture into the tomato shells, piling the prawns up above the rim.
Cut the retained tomato tops into quarters.
Garnish the tomato tops with them &/or small sprigs of parsley.
Serve on a bed of lettuce.

VEGETARIAN SAUCE with PASTA

This is a delicately flavoured dish which stands very well on its own but if you want to, you can add either cooked sausage (warmed and cut into chunks) or cooked ham (diced) at the end. This is a very good compromise if someone wants a vegetarian meal and another wants meat.
Serve with a green salad.

INGREDIENTS

Pasta of choice cooked as per instructions on packet

1 teaspoon olive oil
1 small onion, finely chopped
110 gm (4 oz) sliced mushrooms (fresh or tinned)
3-4 courgettes, cut lengthways then diced
2 generous tablespoons (low fat) crème fraîche
½ teaspoon salt
¼ teaspoon pepper
2 tablespoons grated parmesan cheese

METHOD

In one pan, heat the oil then add the onions, cooking until soft but not brown.
Add the mushrooms, courgettes, salt and pepper and gently simmer with the lid on whilst you cook the pasta. The vegetables should cook without the need to add any other liquid but stir the contents from time to time to ensure the vegetables do not stick to the bottom of the pan and if necessary add a drop of water.
In the second pan, cook the pasta as per packet instructions.
When the pasta is ready, add the crème fraîche to the onion, mushroom & courgette mixture then taste for seasoning.
Drain the pasta then add the onion, mushroom and courgette sauce together with the parmesan cheese and toss well to coat the pasta with the sauce.

Note
If you would like sausages or ham with the dish, add this either to individual servings or in the main dish at the time of serving.

VEGGIE STARTERS

As many of our meals tend to be rice and meat such as curry, chilli, etc., we help our 5-a-day veg. & fruit intake by having starters of green vegetables served with (light) mayonnaise dip.

Asparagus

Cut green beans

METHOD

The method is simple and applies to all the vegetables. **Heat** some water in a pan. **When** boiling, add ½ teaspoon salt and the vegetables.

Broccoli

Cook for 5-10 minutes until the stalks are soft but still firm and can be pierced easily with a sharp knife.
Drain and serve with a (light) mayonnaise dip.

ACKNOWLEDGEMENTS

My grateful thanks to my husband Armand for his encouragement and input into this book, not least for being a very patient taster-in-chief! I am also indebted to him for all the photography and design work - indeed this book is as much his as mine.

I also pay tribute to Kibo, a true gentledog, who died shortly after the photograph shown in the introduction was taken. He also tested and approved the food and for 11 years was a great companion on our travels - we miss him.

It is stated on the verso page that all the recipes in this book were cooked, photographed and consumed in our camper. This is true with the exception of the banana flan, chocolate pots and coffee trifle which because of Armand's dietary restrictions we had to pass over, even though he is by nature a chocoholic. I would therefore like to thank David & Susan Lewis and George and Patricia Hogg, Wardens and Assistant Wardens at Gibson Park Caravan Club Site, Melrose, for coming to the rescue and heroically consuming these deserts in one sitting!

I'd also like to thank Irene Gilkison and Renée Friesner for reading the manuscript and Helena Coryndon for her patient help liasing with the Printers.

*****